The
Science of a
Light Bulb

Neville Evans

WAYLAND

Science World

Other titles in the series:

The Science of
Gravity

The Science of
Noise

The Science of a
Spring

Picture acknowledgements

Wayland Publishers would like to thank the following for allowing their pictures to be reproduced in this book: Martyn F. Chillmaid 8 [top], 13 [bottom]; Eye Ubiquitous/N. Holden 7 [bottom]; Getty Images/Warren Bolster 4, /Ken Briggs 5, /Chad Ehlers 22, /Steven Johnson 16, /H. Richard Johnston 10, /Lenny Kalfus 17 [bottom], /Dennis O'Clair 17 [bottom middle], /Steve Taylor 17 [top middle], 21, 29 [top], /Tek Image *title page*, /Mike Timo 6; Robert Harding *cover* [main], 9 [top], 24, /Louise Murray 26 [top], /Trevor Wood 14; National Portrait Gallery 11; Popperfoto 12, 27 [bottom]; Science Photo Library 13 [top], 15 [both], 23 [top], /Martin Bond 24 [top], 26 [bottom], /Linda Phillips 17 [top], /Charles D. Winters 25; The Stock Market 7 [top], /Roger Ball 23 [bottom]; Trip/A. Lambert 8 [bottom], /Y. Philimoner 11, /H. Rogers 28 [top], /Streano/Havens 27 [top]; Wayland Picture Library *contents page*, *cover* [top and middle], 9 [bottom], 19 [top], 28 [bottom], 29 [bottom]. The chapter logo illustration is by Peter Bull.

Editor: Carron Brown
Consultant: Anne Goldsworthy
Concept design: Lisa Nutt
Designer: Mark Whitchurch
Production controller: Carol Stevens

First published in 1999 by Wayland Publishers Ltd, 61 Western Road, Hove, East Sussex BN3 1JD

British Library in Cataloguing Data
Evans, Neville
 The Science of a Light Bulb. – (Science World)
 1. Light Bulbs – Juvenile literature
 2. Light – Juvenile literature
 I. Title
 535

ISBN 0 7502 2403 7

Find Wayland on the Internet at http://www.wayland.co.uk

Contents

Light before light bulbs

When you go into a dark place, what do you look for first? You look for a light switch to turn on a light. Every day, we use light bulbs to give us instant light at the touch of a switch. At night, you are surrounded by the glow of light bulbs in every building and street. Yet, just over a hundred years ago, light bulbs had not been invented. People had to make light in different ways.

▼ The sun provides us with light and warmth. The sun is a star. Stars make their own heat and light that can travel long distances through space.

Every day has two parts: light and dark, or day and night. At night, we can see many different types of electric light.

Long ago, when the sun went down, there was hardly any light to be seen, except sometimes from the moon. Night was dark, nobody could see and, in many places of the world, it was very, very cold. Heat and light would only come the next day with the rising sun.

▲ The moon doesn't make its own light, like a star. The light we see on the moon's surface is actually reflected sunlight. The light from the sun shines on the moon's surface and bounces down to us on earth.

Burning light

For a long time, people lived using only the sun and moon for light. Then someone, somewhere, at some time, discovered how to make fire. This kept people warm, even when it was dark. People found that fire gave them some light to see during the night. Light from a fire is not as good as sunlight, but it's a lot better than sitting in the dark.

▼ At night, controlled fires are still used on camp sites to give people heat and light.

For many centuries, people made light by burning substances. The most available substance to burn was wood cut from the surrounding trees.

However, people wanted to move around in the dark safely but wood fires had to stay in one place – no one knew how to carry fire. People soon solved this problem by tying wood or other substances, such as cloth or fat, on to sticks that they held above their heads as they walked. These were called torches.

At the start of the Olympic ▶ Games, an athlete lights a torch that burns day and night until the Games finish.

What happens to different materials when a fire gets very hot?

Blacksmiths make horseshoes and gates out of iron, which can be bent into shape when it softens and glows red hot in a fire. When the iron cools, the metal becomes hard again. The colour of burning wood becomes bright red, too. Eventually, it breaks down and becomes ash. Materials, such as paper and cloth, break up into fine ash but metals stay solid (but soften) and change colour.

Lamps

Slowly, people began to learn about other substances that they could burn to give light, such as oil and wax from plants and animals. They learned to control how these substances burned. They kept them in containers, called lamps. The burning substance could be carried safely in a lamp.

Later, people also learned how gases burned to provide heat and light. Gas lamps, gas cooking stoves and gas fires started to be used in buildings to give heat and light. Today, we have gas lamps and stoves to carry around for parties outside. The gas is stored and carried in very strong metal containers (sometimes called 'bottles').

▼ Nineteenth-century miners used oil lamps such as this one to light the dark tunnels where they worked. They now use electric lights.

Which gases are used in gas lamps and stoves?

Butane and propane are the gases used for camp stoves (right) and lights. These gases come from oil in the earth. We get many useful other materials, such as petrol, gasoline and diesel, from oil. All these useful substances are taken out of oil in a place called an oil refinery.

Electricity and light

The electric lamp was invented in 1879. Several people tried to make light using electricity. They knew how lightning during thunderstorms lit up the sky with brilliant flashes of electric light. Some scientists tried to recreate the same effect in laboratories.

In the USA, Benjamin Franklin studied lightning. To lead or conduct electricity to the ground, he flew a kite into a thundercloud. Large, dangerous currents of electricity travelled down the kite string to the ground. Once the electricity hit the ground, it was no longer dangerous. From this experiment, Franklin invented lightning rods to protect buildings from the effects of lightning.

▲ Lightning is an electric flash of light made during a thunderstorm.

Benjamin Franklin

Benjamin Franklin (1706–1790) was an American scientist, politician and inventor. Today, he is best remembered for his invention of lightning rods, which are thick strips of metal strapped to tall buildings, from the top to the bottom. These protect the buildings by 'attracting' and conducting the electricity from lightning safely down to earth.

The arc lamp

In 1808, a young scientist called Humphry Davy invented the arc lamp. This was one successful attempt at recreating lightning. People called it 'lightning on earth'. The arc lamp worked by passing an electric current through two pieces of carbon, a wood-like substance. When the pieces of carbon came close together, they created a bright light.

However, the arc lamp was very dirty, and gave off a lot of smoke and nasty gases. Sometimes it would suddenly stop, plunging everyone into darkness. Despite all this, arc lamps did give out very bright light.

The basic idea of an arc lamp

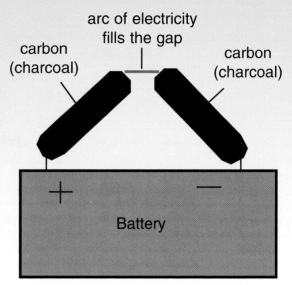

arc of electricity fills the gap

carbon (charcoal)

carbon (charcoal)

+ −

Battery

If the electric current from a battery is powerful enough and the gap between the carbon pieces is small enough, an arc of electricity will jump across the gap forming a bridge of bright light.

◄ Lighthouses used arc lamps until the 1920s. Some combined arc lamps with mirrors to reflect more light out into the sea. Today, lighthouses use powerful electric-filament bulbs which last for longer and are more reliable.

Arc lamps were ▶ used for street lighting in many European and American cities in the late nineteenth century. They were then replaced by electric-filament bulbs.

Sir Humphry Davy

Humphry Davy (1778–1829) was a brilliant chemist who lived in London. He loved experimenting with metals and gases. As well as the electric arc lamp, he also invented the Davy Safety Lamp for use by miners underground. Miners were often afraid of lighting dangerous gases with flames and causing explosions. The safety lamp covered the flame with a wire mesh to stop the gases from being lit. Humphry Davy was also a poet and a very popular public speaker.

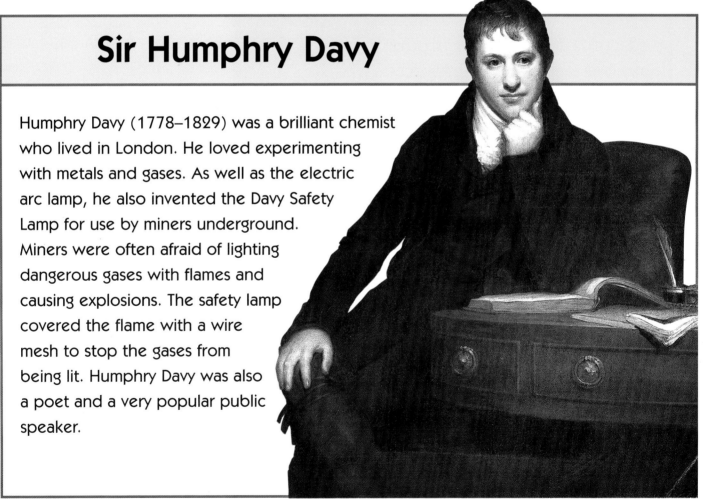

Problems to be solved

No one could rely on an arc lamp to produce bright light for long. Many scientists around the world investigated other ways of making bright light using electricity.

Thomas Alva Edison

Thomas Alva Edison (1847–1931) was the most famous American inventor experimenting with electric light. He discovered that when he connected substances to a battery, they usually heated up. If he used more batteries, and therefore more power, the substances would become red and sometimes even white with heat. However, the substances only lasted for a short time before they broke up. Edison tried using different substances, such as paper, wood and even corn! He found that metals lasted longer than other substances.

Sir Joseph Wilson Swan

Sir Joseph Wilson Swan (1828–1914), was an English chemist who experimented with electric light. His designs influenced Edison's final bulbs. Both Edison and Swan set up companies to provide electric lighting throughout their countries. Swan also made important discoveries in photography.

The first problem for the scientists was that their electric lamps were not reliable – at one moment there would be bright light, the next moment darkness. Obviously these lamps would be no use for houses and streets as they would need to be checked all the time.

The main part of the lamp (the metal carrying the electric current) was exposed to the open air which caused it to heat up very fast and melt. So, how could this problem be solved? Simple, cover the metal up! But surely if it was covered up, the light wouldn't be seen. However, if the cover was made of something that the light could go through, such as glass, the light would be seen.

Substances that let light ▶ through, such as glass and some plastics, are called transparent. Can you think of any glass objects that you look through? For example, you can look through windows and glass over pictures.

Edison's glass bulb

Edison decided to experiment with lighting metal substances inside a glass bulb. He hoped that the bulb would help the hot metal give light for longer.

Edison was right, it did work much better, but the design still needed a lot of work. The inside of the bulb became very black – not much use for letting light through it.

After many attempts and failures, Edison wondered whether the air inside the bulb was part of the problem. When the metal in the bulb got hot, the air caused it to heat up too fast. So, Edison pumped most of the air from inside the bulb and the metal heated more slowly – the light lasted for a longer time. This was the first step to the electric light bulb.

▼ People have made objects by heating and softening glass for many years.

This is an illustration of one of the first light bulbs ▶ designed by Edison in 1880. It took Edison 6,000 tries to find a light bulb that would keep the electric light working without constant supervision.

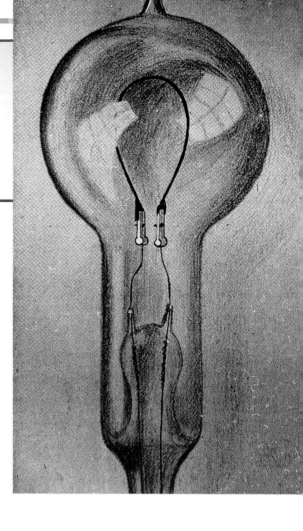

Success!

Finally, in 1879, Edison made an electric lamp that stayed on for several minutes. He was highly delighted. Can you imagine anyone being happy about a light that stayed on for a few minutes? Today, we have lights that stay on for days and days.

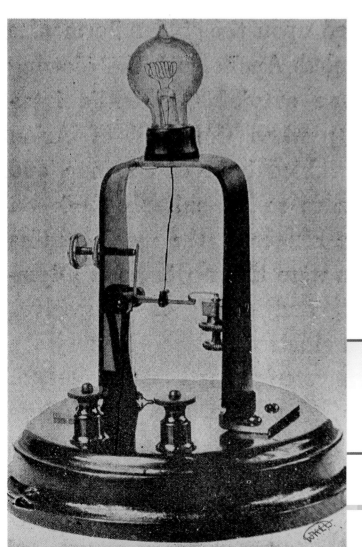

But, remember, no one else before Edison had ever got a lamp to stay lit for more than a few minutes. Without Edison's work, and that of Swan, we might not have our modern, reliable light bulbs.

◀ This illustration shows the first electric lamp with a light bulb, designed by Edison in 1879.

Filaments

Edison found that thick pieces of metal did not work for his bulbs. Instead, he made the metal extremely thin, as thin as a piece of cotton thread. These pieces of metal are called filaments, from the Latin word for 'thread'. Edison's electric-filament bulbs are still in use today, all over the world.

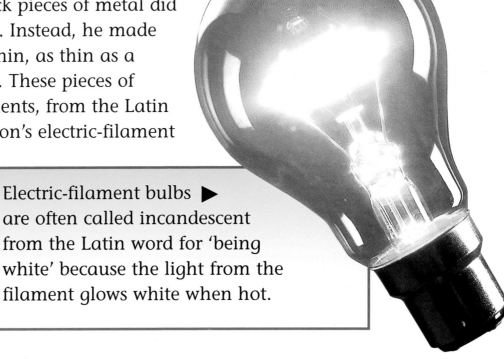

Electric-filament bulbs ▶ are often called incandescent from the Latin word for 'being white' because the light from the filament glows white when hot.

A simple plan of how an electric-filament bulb lights

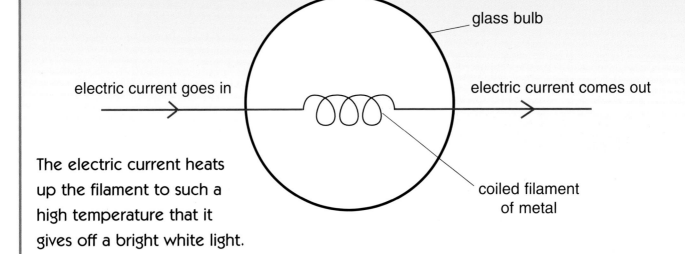

glass bulb

electric current goes in

electric current comes out

The electric current heats up the filament to such a high temperature that it gives off a bright white light.

coiled filament of metal

Before scientists found the perfect filament for Edison's bulb, they had many questions to answer. Today, we know the answers to the questions:

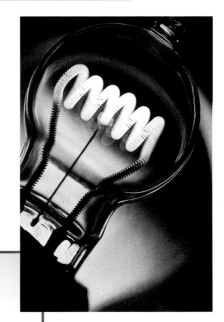

Q. Which metal should a filament be made from?
A. The best metal to use is called tungsten, which produces a very bright white light and doesn't melt as soon as other metals.

Q. Is a straight filament better or worse than a coiled filament?
A. A coiled filament is better than a straight one because it lasts longer.

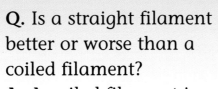

Q. How hot should a filament be?
A. The filament needs to be at a temperature of more than 2,000°C.

Q. Would it be better to have a small amount of gas inside a bulb rather than no gas at all?
A. It is better to have a small amount of the gases argon and nitrogen inside a bulb because they prevent the filament from heating up too fast.

Electric circuits

Many items of electricity in your house can be plugged into sockets in the walls. Behind the walls are wires that connect to each other and to the electricity supply which makes the electric switches work. This system of wires with the electricity supply is called an electric circuit.

One way to understand how light bulbs, switches and electricity are all linked together is to look at simple electric circuits.

Some symbols used in electric circuits

A light bulb is shown by this symbol:

A switch is shown by this symbol:

The wire that joins the parts of a circuit together is shown by a line:

A battery, which supplies the electric current, is shown by this symbol:

The simplest circuit is this one:

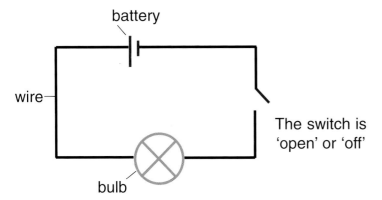

The switch is 'open' or 'off'

The switch is open (off) so there is a gap or break in the circuit. The gap is too large for the electric current to jump across, so there is no flow of electricity through the bulb and therefore no light.

▲ If you make the simplest circuit and press the switch on, the bulb will light.

What are voltage numbers?

Voltage numbers indicate the electric 'strength', e.g. 2 volt or 2V, of an object. Each battery and bulb has a voltage number. The voltage numbers on the bulb and battery must be the same if the bulb is to light. If the battery voltage is much lower than the bulb needs, the filament of the bulb will only glow a dull red. If the battery voltage is much higher, the filament will glow a very bright white for a short time, then it will break and be of no further use.

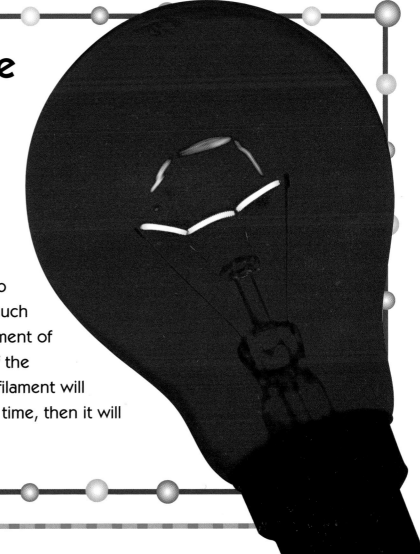

More complicated circuits

It is possible to have different numbers of batteries, bulbs and switches in one circuit and change their positions. The diagrams below show some circuits with more parts to them.

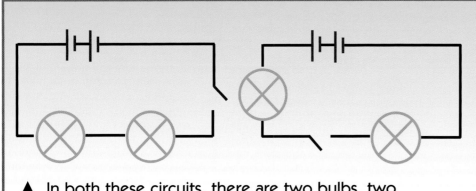

▲ In both these circuits, there are two bulbs, two batteries and one switch. When the switches are pressed on, the circuits will be complete and the bulbs will light.

Warning!

Be very careful not to touch lights that have been on for several minutes or longer. They are very hot to touch and can cause a nasty burn.

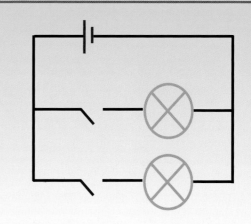

▲ In this circuit, there are two switches, two bulbs and one battery. If you press one of the switches on, only one part of the circuit is complete and only one of the bulbs will light.

Electric circuits at home

The circuit in your home is bigger and very dangerous compared to a simple circuit. Instead of small batteries close to you, the circuits are powered by big electric power stations far away that provide electricity at high voltages to your home through large cables.

In buildings, it isn't possible to see all parts of a circuit because most of it is hidden behind walls, above the ceiling or under the floor. So, the only parts of a circuit that we see in a room are power sockets, light switches, wires and light bulbs.

How does the electric current flow into and out of a bulb?

An electric current has to flow through a bulb so it will light. The bulb screws into a special holder to keep it upright and to make sure that the flow of current is right. There are two types of light bulb fittings (the bit that fits into a bulb holder): bayonet and screw. Each fitting has a different way of leading the current through it.

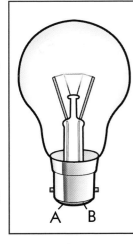

◄ The bayonet fitting has two metal points at the side that fit into the holder. The electric current flows in at point A. It then flows through the filament and out at point B.

◄ The metal screw fitting screws into the holder. The electric current flows in at point A. It then flows through the filament and out at point B.

Modern lighting

Today, we have many different 'artificial' lights. These lights are not natural, like sunlight, because they are made by people or machines in factories. No artificial lights are as good as sunlight, but their development in the past century has changed everyday life for the better. We use lights every day for many reasons. We use light to drive and walk safely at night, read, shop, light up buildings and even to see in the fridge.

Think about all the hundreds even thousands of lights you see at night over a town. In order for these lights to be working at the same time, a special system is used to generate enough electricity. No battery is big enough. The electricity comes from an electric generator in a power station.

▼ The glow of thousands of lights all over this city is produced by electricity from a power station.

Michael Faraday

Michael Faraday (1791–1867) worked on electromagnetism and other topics at The Royal Institution, London. He was a very clever scientist but a little shy. He loved speaking to audiences of young people. Without his discoveries of electromagnetism, none of the lighting systems we depend on today would be possible.

The generator works because there is a close link between electricity and magnetism, called electromagnetism. Most of the early research on this topic was done by Michael Faraday, who became known as 'the father of electricity'. Faraday discovered that when a coil of wire spins very fast between the poles of a magnet, big voltages and large electric currents are generated. This is electromagnetism.

These men are inspecting the blades ▶ of a generator. Generators are large machines in a power station. They are forced by the motion of steam or water to spin round very fast. This generates the large voltages of electricity that power our homes.

◀ Power stations are situated just outside towns and cities. The powerful machines inside them can generate enough electricity to power the surrounding area.

How does electricity get from the power station to my house?

The voltages generated in the power stations are so high and dangerous that they have to be carried to the surrounding towns by thick cables. You have probably seen large metal pylons (right) in the country which carry electric cables. In towns, electric cables are also covered by insulating material (to stop the electricity passing through the cable into anything or anyone touching it) and buried underground.

Most lights in houses still use Edison's type of electric light (a very hot filament inside a glass bulb). However, they have one weakness. They generate a lot of heat as well as light. In nature, when you get light, you get heat; think about fires, or the sun. The heat given off by a light bulb is a waste because it doesn't help you see any better.

Fluorescent lighting

In the 1950s, after a lot of experimenting, scientists succeeded in setting up a new type of electric light, called a fluorescent tube. This new long and thin light didn't look at all like the first light bulbs. The glass tube was filled with a gas and didn't need a metal filament. There are usually two gases inside the tube: argon and mercury vapour.

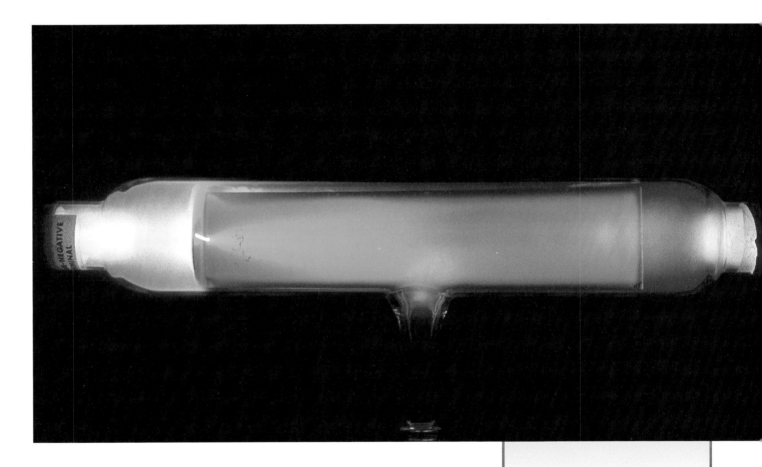

In order to make the light even brighter, the inside surface of the tube is painted with a substance called phosphor. Some people have described fluorescent lighting as 'lightning in a bottle'. Look out for fluorescent tube lighting around you today – you will see it in many places.

▲ Fluorescent lights can be different colours depending on what type of gas is used in each tube.

◀ Fluorescent lighting is usually whiter than the light from filament lights. It is used in offices, factories and shops where spaces need to be lit with a light similar to daylight.

The importance of fluorescent tube lights is that they don't get as hot as filament lights for the same power. This means they do not drain as much energy from a power station and they are much cheaper to use than filament bulbs. Modern fluorescent lights are all designed to save energy in homes and in workplaces. They last eight times longer than filament bulbs but produce the same amount of light.

These modern fluorescent lights ▶ show how the design from the long thin tubes fifty years ago has changed. The tubes have become smaller and can be used in the same fittings as filament bulbs.

One filament or fluorescent light gives a lot of light in small spaces, such as rooms in a house or on a table or beside your bed. However, one light does not give enough light to cover larger distances, so several lights are needed on streets or along corridors. For greater brightness, other types of lights are needed. These lights are used in stadiums, large car parks, hospital operating theatres, television studios and in lighthouses. Their brightness is needed for three reasons: to make places safe; so that light can be seen from far away; or to give a clear picture of small detail.

All electric lamps are basically developments of the filament or arc lamp. So, a big thank you to all the scientists who helped invent our modern lighting.

▲ Very powerful lights are needed to light up stadiums. Though they're meant to light up only the inside of the stadium, people can see the glow of the lights from far away.

◀ Many lights are needed to light up long corridors. This exhibition centre is using many different lights to decorate the corridor.

More points about light

1. Light starts out from something. We call this a source. The biggest source that we are familiar with is our sun.

Warning!

Never look directly at the sun, especially with binoculars or a telescope. The sun's light is so strong that it could damage your eyes very badly.

2. Light from a source travels in all directions. If we are to see, the light must travel into our eyes.

3. Our eyes are not sources of light. Light goes into our eyes. There has to be light so that we can see anything. Our eyes cannot see in total darkness.

4. Other sources of light are electric lights, candles and fires. Some living creatures generate their own light, such as fireflies.

5. Light from sources travels around and hits objects in the way. Sometimes it goes through the object, if the object is transparent. All these objects are transparent.

6. If an object is not transparent, it is called opaque. Light 'bounces off' opaque objects (this is sometimes called reflection and sometimes scattering).

7. 'Bouncing off' enables us to see things. This is how you are able to read this sentence. The light from some sources (the sun in daytime, your lamp at night) hits this page and then 'bounces off' into your eye.

8. Reflections: in very special cases, the effect of 'bouncing off' is stunning. You can see yourself in a surface if the surface in shiny, like a mirror. You can have all sorts of fun in mirrors of different sorts. Silvery or shiny surfaces are best for reflection. Any shiny surface will do. Look around for some and then look at your reflection in them.

Glossary

Battery An object that can store electricity and can be used to power electrical devices.

Circuits The paths of electric currents.

Conduct To lead or guide.

Electric currents The flow of electricity through, for example, a wire.

Electricity An invisible form of energy that is used to make light and heat, and to power machinery.

Electromagnetism Energy that combines electricity and magnetic energies.

Energy Energy makes things work.

Filament A thread-like piece of metal used in a light bulb to give light when an electric current passes through it.

Gases Substances that are neither solid nor liquid, like oxygen in air. Some gases burn to produce heat and light.

Insulating Covering bare electrical wire with a material, e.g. plastic or rubber, which electricity will not pass through to harm anyone touching it.

Laboratories Places where scientists carry out experiments.

Lightning A large electric flash during a thunderstorm.

Miners People who work underground to dig out substances such as coal.

Natural Having something to do with nature; not artificial.

Oil refinery A place where oil is separated into several pure substances, such as petrol and diesel.

Opaque Objects that do not let light pass through. The opposite of transparent.

Reflected When light has bounced off an opaque object, reflecting images into your eye.

Socket A hole or hollow place that something is fitted into, e.g. an electric light socket.

Stoves Metal objects that can give heat for cooking or for warming a room.

Switch A small lever or button that turns an electric current on or off.

Transparent Objects that let light pass through.

Vapour A gas form of a substance that is usually solid or liquid, e.g. mercury.

Voltages Electrical forces measured in volts.

Volts The units used for measuring the force of electricity.

Further Information

Books to read

Batteries, Bulbs and Wires
by David Glover (Kingfisher, 1999)

The Bright Idea – The Story of Thomas Edison by Ann Moore (Macdonald Young Books, 1997)

Electricity (*Science Workshop* series)
by Peter Robson (Watts, 1995)

Electricity (*Straightforward Science* series) by Peter Riley (Watts, 1998)

Light (*Focus On* series)
by Barbara Taylor (Watts, 1992)

Light (*Science Projects* series)
by Trevor Day (Wayland, 1997)

Websites to visit

www.nmsi.ac.uk/welcome.html
The home page of the Science Museum, London.

www.askeric.org/Projects/Newton
This site contains many interesting science lessons.

www.exploratory.org.uk
You can find your nearest hands-on science centre at this site.

Places of interest

The Science Museum, Exhibition Road,
South Kensington, London
(Tel: 0207 938 8000).

Michael Faraday's Laboratory and Museum
The Royal Institution, 21 Albemarle Street,
London W1X 4BS (Tel: 0207 409 2992)

See 'websites to visit' (above) for information on where to find your nearest hands-on science centre.

Light Bulb
TOPIC WEB

GEOGRAPHY
- Find out where your nearest power station is and make a map of the area it supplies electricity to.
- Look at your local area and draw a map showing how light bulbs are used, e.g. street lights, signs, in houses.

HISTORY
- Read more about the lives of Edison, Swan, Davy and Faraday. Discover why they made their inventions.
- Look at the design of street and house lights in the past 100 years.

MATHS
- Investigate how many light bulbs are used in different places, such as your house, a friend's house, your school, library, factory. Then make a graph to compare your information.

ART
- Look at how light has been used in art, e.g. stained-glass windows, Tiffany lamp shades.

DESIGN AND TECHNOLOGY
- Investigate the different needs for light in your house and other buildings, e.g. having a light in the fridge.
- Look at how different light bulbs and lights are designed to show light in different ways.

Science
- Discover and compare different light sources.
- Investigate the tricks of light: e.g. shadows, reflections, rainbows.
- Look at how electric circuits and electricity works using simple circuits. Always remember to use batteries and follow safety instructions.
- Look at your reflection in different surfaces and compare your results.

ENGLISH
- Imagine you are in the 19th century. Write a newspaper article about Edison's new light bulbs, or interview your friend, who is playing the part of Edison.

Index

Numbers in **bold** refer to pictures as well as text.